Simone Biles Biography For Kids

The Exciting Tale of America's greatest gymnast of all time, A little Golden book biography to inspire new readers to give them courage to soar and become big dremers

Academic Press

Table of contents

1. Introduction

Have you ever wondered what it takes to become the best gymnast in the world? How about the best gymnast of all time?

If you have, then you will love this book about Simone Biles, the amazing athlete who has achieved more than anyone else in the history of gymnastics.

Simone Biles was not born with a silver spoon in her mouth. She had to overcome many challenges and hardships in her life, from being adopted by her grandparents, to being bullied at school, to facing racism and sexism in her sport.

But Simone did not let anything stop her from pursuing her passion and her dreams. She worked hard, trained hard, and believed in herself. She also had a lot of fun along the way, making friends, enjoying music, and expressing her personality.

In this book, you will learn all about Simone's incredible journey, from her humble beginnings in Texas, to her dazzling performances at the Olympics, to her inspiring role as a leader and a voice for change. You will also discover some of the secrets behind her amazing skills, such as how she does the "Biles", a move so difficult that no one else can do it.

This book is more than just a biography. It is a story of courage, perseverance, and joy. It is a story of how one girl defied the odds and became a legend. It is a story that will inspire you to follow your own dreams, whatever they may be.

Are you ready to meet Simone Biles, the unbelievable story of America's greatest gymnast of all time? Then grab this book and let's go!

2. Early Years

- Birth and Family with Childhood and Early Interests

Simone Biles was born on March 14, 1997, in Columbus, Ohio. She is the third of four children of Shanon Biles, who struggled with drug and alcohol addiction. Simone and her siblings often faced hunger, neglect, and abuse in their unstable home.

When Simone was three years old, she and her sister Adria were placed in foster care. They moved from one foster home to another, feeling unwanted and unloved. Simone later said, \"I was so young, I didn't quite understand what was going on.

But everything changed when Simone was five years old. Her maternal grandparents, Ronald and Nellie Biles, decided to adopt Simone and Adria and bring them to their home in Spring, Texas. Ronald and Nellie became Simone's new parents, and she started calling them \"Dad\" and \"Mom\". Simone also gained two older brothers, Ronald

Jr. and Adam, who were Ronald's sons from a previous marriage.

Simone finally found a loving and supportive family that gave her a sense of belonging and security. She said, \"My parents saved me. They've set huge examples of how to treat other people, and they've been there to support me since day one.

Simone's new life in Texas was full of joy and adventure. She loved playing with her sister and brothers, riding bikes, climbing trees, and jumping on the trampoline. She also enjoyed watching cartoons, listening to music, and reading books. She is a curious and energetic child who always wanted to learn new things and have fun.

One of the things that Simone learned and had fun with was gymnastics. She is introduced to the sport when She is six years old, during a field trip to Bannon's Gymnastix. She is amazed by the gymnasts who flipped and twisted in the air, and she wanted to try it herself. She asked her mom if she could enroll in a gymnastics class, and her mom agreed.

Simone soon discovered that she had a natural talent and passion for gymnastics. She progressed quickly, mastering skills that took other gymnasts years to learn. She also developed a fearless and confident attitude, always willing to take on new challenges and push her limits. She said, \"I don't think of the difficulty. I just think of the fun.

Simone's coaches recognized her potential and encouraged her to pursue her dreams. When She is eight years old, she joined the competitive team at Bannon's Gymnastix, where she trained under Aimee Boorman. Boorman became Simone's mentor and friend, guiding her through the ups and downs of her gymnastics career.

Simone's early years were filled with hardships and happiness, challenges and achievements, struggles and triumphs. They shaped her into the person and the gymnast she would become. They prepared her for the amazing journey that lay ahead of her. A journey that would make her the greatest gymnast of all time.

3. Discovering Gymnastics

- First Encounter with Gymnastics

Simone Biles had no idea what gymnastics was until She is six years old. That was when she went on a field trip with her daycare to Bannon's Gymnastix, a local gym in Houston, Texas. There, she saw something that changed her life forever.

She saw gymnasts of all ages and levels, doing amazing things on different apparatuses. She saw them swinging on bars, balancing on beams, vaulting over tables, and tumbling on mats. She saw them flipping and twisting in the air, landing with grace and power. She saw them smiling and cheering, having fun and making friends. She saw them wearing colorful leotards, shiny medals, and sparkling ribbons. She saw them as stars.

Simone was mesmerized by what she saw. She felt a surge of excitement and curiosity. She wanted to be like them. She wanted to do what they did. She wanted to try gymnastics.

She asked her mom, Nellie, if she could join a gymnastics class. Nellie agreed, thinking it would be a good way for Simone to burn off some of her extra energy and learn some discipline. She did not know that She is giving Simone the best gift ever. She did not know that She is opening the door to Simone's destiny.

Simone enrolled in a beginner class at Bannon's Gymnastix, where she met her coach, Aimee Boorman. Aimee was a young and friendly woman who loved gymnastics and teaching kids. She noticed something special about Simone right away. She noticed that Simone had a natural talent and passion for gymnastics. She noticed that Simone learned new skills quickly and easily. She noticed that Simone was fearless and confident, always willing to take on new challenges and push her limits. She noticed that Simone was a star in the making.

Aimee became Simone's mentor and friend, guiding her through the ups and downs of her gymnastics career. She taught Simone the basics of gymnastics, such as how to stretch, warm up, and cool down. She taught Simone the rules and etiquette of gymnastics, such as how to salute the judges, respect the coaches, and support the teammates. She taught Simone the skills and routines of gymnastics, such as how to do a cartwheel, a handstand, and a round-off. She taught Simone the joy and beauty of gymnastics, such as how to express herself, have fun, and be creative. She taught Simone how to be a gymnast.

Simone loved gymnastics more than anything. She loved the feeling of flying and spinning in the air. She loved the challenge of learning new and harder skills. She loved the thrill of competing and winning. She loved the camaraderie of being part of a team. She loved the satisfaction of achieving her goals. She loved the dream of becoming the best. She loved gymnastics with all her heart.

Simone's first encounter with gymnastics was the start of an incredible journey. A journey that would take her to places she never imagined. A journey that would make her the greatest gymnast of all time. A journey that would inspire millions of people around the world. .

- Early Gymnastics Training

Simone's coach, Aimee Boorman, saw her potential and encouraged her to join the competitive team. She also became Simone's mentor and friend, guiding her through the ups and downs of her gymnastics career. Aimee taught Simone not only the basics of gymnastics, but also the joy and beauty of it. She helped Simone express herself, have fun, and be creative. She also helped Simone develop a fearless and confident attitude, always willing to take on new challenges and push her limits.

Simone started competing at the age of eight, and she soon showed that She is a star in the making. She won her first gold medal in floor exercise at the Women's Junior Olympic National Championships in 2010, when She is 13 years old. She also won a bronze medal in vault at the same competition. She is amazed and proud of her achievements, and she wanted to keep improving and winning.

Simone continued to train hard and progress fast, mastering skills that took other gymnasts years to learn. She also developed her own signature moves, such as the "Biles", a double layout with a half twist and a blind landing on floor exercise. She is not afraid to try new and harder skills, and she always amazed the judges and the audience with her power and grace.

Simone's early gymnastics training was not easy. She had to balance her schoolwork, her family life, and her social life with her rigorous training schedule. She also had to deal with injuries, setbacks, and pressures. She sometimes felt tired, frustrated, and nervous. But she never gave up. She always found a way to overcome her challenges and keep her passion alive. She always had the support of her coach, her family, and her friends. She always had the dream of becoming the best. She always had the love of gymnastics.

Simone's early gymnastics training was the foundation of her success. It was the time when she discovered her talent and passion for the sport. It was the time when she learned the skills and the routines that would make her a champion. . .

4. Rising Star

- *Joining the Gymnastics Scene*

Elite gymnastics is the level where gymnasts compete for national and international titles, and where they can qualify for the Olympics and the World Championships. Elite gymnastics is also the level where the competition is fierce, the pressure is high, and the expectations are huge. Elite gymnastics is not for the faint of heart.

Simone knew that elite gymnastics was her dream, and She is determined to pursue it. She had been working hard with her coach, Aimee Boorman, to prepare for the challenge. She had been learning new and harder skills, such as the double-twisting double back on floor exercise, and the Amanar on vault, a two-and-a-half twisting Yurchenko. She had also been improving her artistry, flexibility, and consistency. She is ready to show the world what she could do.

Simone's first elite competition was the American Classic, a qualifier for the US Classic, the traditional tune-up event before the US National Championships. Simone needed to score at least 52 points in the all-around to qualify for the US Classic, and she did it with ease. She scored 56.7 points, the highest score of the day, and won the all-around title by more than four points. She also won the gold medals on vault, beam, and floor, and the silver medal on bars. She impressed everyone with her power, grace, and confidence. She made a statement: She is a rising star.

Simone's next elite competition was the US Classic, where she faced some of the best gymnasts in the country, including the reigning Olympic champion, Gabby Douglas, and the reigning world champion, Jordyn Wieber. Simone was not intimidated by the competition. She is excited to compete with them and learn from them. She said, \"I'm just here to have fun and do the best I can.

Simone did more than just have fun and do her best. She stunned the gymnastics world with her performance. She scored 60.45 points in the all-around, the highest score ever recorded at the US Classic, and won the all-around title by more than three points. She also won the gold medals on vault and floor, and the bronze medals on beam and bars.

She dazzled the judges and the audience with her skills, such as the Biles on floor, a double layout with a half twist and a blind landing, a move so difficult that no one else could do it. She also showed her personality, smiling and dancing throughout her routines. She won the hearts of the fans, who cheered and chanted her name. She made history: She is a superstar.

Simone's first elite season was a huge success. She qualified for the US National Championships, where she would compete for the chance to represent the United States at the World Championships in Tokyo, Japan. She also earned the respect and admiration of her peers, her coaches, and the gymnastics community. She proved that She is not just a talented gymnast, but also a hard-working, humble, and joyful person. She proved that She is not just a rising star, but also a shining star. A star that would light up the gymnastics scene for years to come. . . .

- Notable Achievements in Junior Competitions

She trained and competed in gymnastics for a few years, but She is still relatively unknown to the wider gymnastics world. That changed in 2012, when she made her mark in the junior national and international competitions, winning medals and titles that showcased her talent and potential.

Simone's first domestic wins came in 2012, when she captured the junior all-around crowns at both the American and U.S. Classic competitions, catching the eye of many in the sport for her powerful tumbling and performance on vault, where her Yurchenko two-and-a-half dazzled. She also won the gold medals on floor exercise and balance beam at both events, and the silver medal on uneven bars at the U.S. Classic. She impressed everyone with her consistency, artistry, and confidence. She made a statement: She is a rising star.

Simone's next challenge was the U.S. National Championships, where she faced some of the best junior gymnasts in the country, including Katelyn Ohashi, the reigning junior world champion. Simone was not intimidated by the competition. She is excited to compete with them and learn from them. She said, \"I just wanted to go out there and have fun and hit four for four.

Simone did more than just have fun and hit four for four. She dominated the competition with her performance. She scored 60.85 points in the all-around, the highest score ever recorded by a junior gymnast at the U.S. National Championships, and won the all-around title by more than three points. She also won the gold medals on vault, floor exercise, and balance beam, and the bronze medal on uneven bars. She dazzled the judges and the audience with her skills, such as the Biles on floor, a double layout with a half twist and a blind landing, a move so difficult that no one else could do it. She also showed her personality, smiling and dancing throughout her routines. She won the hearts of the fans, who cheered and chanted her name. She made history: She is a superstar.

Simone's first international win came in 2012, when she represented the United States at the Pacific Rim Championships in Everett, Washington. She competed alongside senior gymnasts, such as Aly Raisman and Jordyn Wieber, who would later become her teammates and friends at the 2016 Olympics. Simone held her own against the older and more experienced gymnasts, and helped the U.S. team win the gold medal. She also won the silver medal in the junior all-around competition, behind Ohashi, and the gold medal on vault. She proved that she could compete at the highest level of gymnastics, and that She is ready for the next step. She proved that She is not just a rising star, but also a shining star. A star that would light up the gymnastics scene for years to come. .

5. Facing Challenges

- Overcoming Obstacles

She had to deal with injuries, setbacks, pressures, and expectations that threatened to derail her dreams. She also had to cope with personal traumas, such as being a survivor of sexual abuse by former USA Gymnastics team doctor Larry Nassar, and losing her brother to a murder charge. She had to overcome not only physical and mental challenges, but also emotional and social ones.

But Simone did not let anything stop her from pursuing her passion and her goals. She showed remarkable resilience, determination, and courage in the face of adversity. She used various strategies to overcome her obstacles, such as:

- Seeking help and support from her coach, her family, her friends, and her therapist. She learned to trust and rely on the people who cared about her and wanted her to succeed. She also learned to speak up and share her feelings and thoughts with others, instead of bottling them up inside. She said, \"It's OK to get help if you need it.

- Practicing self-care and mindfulness. She learned to take care of her body and mind, by eating well, sleeping well, resting well, and meditating. She also learned to focus on the present moment, instead of worrying about the past or the future. She said, \"I try to stay in tune with my body and be mentally strong.

- Finding joy and fun in gymnastics. She learned to enjoy the sport and the process, instead of stressing over the results and the outcomes. She also learned to express herself and her personality through her routines, and to have fun and be creative. She said, \"I love gymnastics. It makes me happy. I like to show the world who I am.

- Believing in herself and her abilities. She learned to have confidence and faith in herself, and to trust her instincts and decisions. She also learned to embrace her strengths and weaknesses, and to celebrate her achievements and learn from her mistakes. She said, \"I know what I'm capable of. I just have to go out there and do it.

Simone's overcoming of obstacles was not easy. It took a lot of hard work, patience, and courage. It also took a lot of trial and error, and learning and growing. But she never gave up. She always found a way to overcome her challenges and keep her passion alive. She always had the support of her coach, her family, and her friends. She always had the dream of becoming the best. She always had the love of gymnastics.

Simone's overcoming of obstacles was the key to her success. It was the time when she showed her resilience, determination, and courage. It was the time when she learned the skills and the strategies that would help her cope with any situation.

- Building Mental Toughness

She had to deal with the pressure of being the best, the expectations of others, and the criticism of herself. She also had to cope with the stress of competing at the highest level, the fear of failure, and the uncertainty of the future. She had to overcome not only physical and technical difficulties, but also psychological and emotional ones.

But Simone did not let these challenges break her. She used them to make her stronger. She developed a mindset and a set of strategies that helped her build her mental toughness. She learned to:

- Set realistic and attainable goals. She learned to focus on what she could control, such as her effort, attitude, and performance, rather than what she could not, such as the scores, the judges, and the outcomes. She also learned to break down her big goals into smaller and more manageable ones, and to celebrate her progress and achievements along the way. She said, \"I don't focus on the medals. I focus on the process.

- Embrace challenges and learn from mistakes. She learned to see challenges as opportunities to grow and improve, rather than as threats or obstacles. She also learned to accept and learn from her mistakes, rather than to avoid or dwell on them. She said, \"I don't think of it as a failure. I think of it as a lesson.

- Stay positive and optimistic. She learned to feed her mind with positive thoughts and affirmations, rather than with negative ones. She also learned to look at the bright side of things, and to expect the best, rather than the worst. She said, \"I always try to think positive and tell myself I can do it.

- Seek support and feedback. She learned to trust and rely on the people who cared about her and wanted her to succeed, such as her coach, her family, her friends, and her therapist. She also learned to seek and listen to constructive feedback, rather than to ignore or reject it. She said, \"I have a great support system that helps me through the tough times.

Simone's building of mental toughness was not easy. It took a lot of hard work, patience, and courage. It also took a lot of trial and error, and learning and growing. But she never gave up. She always found a way to build her mental toughness and keep her passion alive. She always had the support of her coach, her family, and her friends. She always had the dream of becoming the best. She always had the love of gymnastics.

Simone's building of mental toughness was the key to her success. It was the time when she showed her resilience, determination, and courage. It was the time when she learned the skills and the strategies that would help her cope with any situation. It was the time when she became a role model and a leader for others.

6. Road to Excellence

- Transition to Senior Competitions

She is dominating the junior level of gymnastics, winning medals and titles that showcased her talent and potential. But she knew that the real challenge was ahead of her: the senior level, where she would face the best gymnasts in the world, and where she would have the chance to compete at the Olympics and the World Championships.

Simone was ready to make the transition to the senior level in 2014, when she turned 18 years old. She had been working hard with her coach, Aimee Boorman, to prepare for the new level of difficulty and intensity. She had been adding new and harder skills to her routines, such as the Cheng on vault, a round-off half-on, one-and-a-half twist off, and the double-double on floor, a double back with two twists. She had also been improving her artistry, execution, and consistency. She is confident and excited to show the world what she could do.

Simone's first senior competition was the American Cup, an invitational event that featured some of the top gymnasts from around the world, such as Kyla Ross from the United States, Larisa Iordache from Romania, and Vanessa Ferrari from Italy. Simone was not intimidated by the competition. She is eager to compete with them and learn from them. She said, \"I'm just here to have fun and do my best.

Simone did more than just have fun and do her best. She blew away the competition with her performance. She scored 61.132 points in the all-around, the highest score ever recorded at the American Cup, and won the all-around title by more than four points. She also won the gold medals on vault, beam, and floor, and the silver medal on bars. She amazed the judges and the audience with her skills, such as the Biles on floor, a double layout with a half twist and a blind landing, a move so difficult that no one else could do it. She also showed her personality, smiling and dancing throughout her routines. She won the hearts of the fans, who cheered and chanted her name. She made history: She is a superstar.

Simone's next challenge was the U.S. National Championships, where she faced some of the best senior gymnasts in the country, including the reigning Olympic champion, Gabby Douglas, and the reigning world champion, Jordyn Wieber. Simone was not intimidated by the competition. She is excited to compete with them and learn from them. She said, \"I just want to go out there and hit four for four.

Simone did more than just hit four for four. She dominated the competition with her performance. She scored 122.55 points in the all-around, the highest score ever recorded by a senior gymnast at the U.S. National Championships, and won the all-around title by more than three points. She also won the gold medals on vault, beam, and floor, and the bronze medal on bars. She dazzled the judges and the audience with her skills, such as the Cheng on vault, a move so difficult that only a few gymnasts in the world could do it. She also showed her personality, smiling and dancing throughout her routines. She won the hearts of the fans, who cheered and chanted her name. She made history: She is a superstar.

Simone's first senior season was a huge success. She qualified for the World Championships in Nanning, China, where she would compete for the chance to become the world champion. She also earned the respect and admiration of her peers, her coaches, and the gymnastics community. She proved that She is not just a talented gymnast, but also a hard-working, humble, and joyful person. She proved that She is not just a rising star, but also a shining star. A star that would light up the gymnastics scene for years to come.

- Dominating the Gymnastics World

She wanted to be great. She wanted to be the best. She wanted to dominate the gymnastics world.

And that's exactly what she did. From 2014 to 2019, Simone Biles became the most dominant gymnast in history, winning every major competition she entered, and breaking records left and right. She won six world all-around titles, the most by any gymnast, male or female. She won 19 world gold medals, the most by any gymnast, male or female. She won 25 world medals, the most by any gymnast, male or female. She won four Olympic gold medals, the most by any American gymnast in a single Games. She won the Laureus World Sportswoman of the Year award twice, the only gymnast to do so. She won the hearts and minds of millions of fans around the world, who admired her skills, her personality, and her courage. She made history: She is a legend.

Simone Biles dominated the gymnastics world with her extraordinary achievements, performances, and milestones. She achieved feats that no one else had ever done, or even attempted, such as the Biles II on floor, a triple-twisting double back, and the Biles on beam, a double-twisting double back dismount. She performed routines that were so difficult and complex, that they had the highest difficulty scores in the sport, and that only she could execute with such power and grace. She reached milestones that were so impressive and unprecedented, that they earned her a place in the history books, and in the hearts of many. She did all this with a smile on her face, a sparkle in her eyes, and a joy in her heart. She did all this with a passion and a purpose, a determination and a drive, a confidence and a courage. She did all this with a love of gymnastics.

Simone Biles dominated the gymnastics world, but she also changed it. She changed the way people saw gymnastics, as a sport that was not only about precision and perfection, but also about creativity and expression. She changed the way people saw gymnasts, as athletes who were not only strong and skilled, but also human and vulnerable. She changed the way people saw themselves, as individuals who were not only capable of achieving their goals, but also worthy of pursuing their dreams. She inspired millions of people around the world, especially young girls and women, to follow their passions, to overcome their challenges, to embrace their strengths, and to celebrate their differences. She inspired millions of people around the world, to be themselves, to be brave, to be bold, to be Biles.

7. Olympic Dreams

- First Olympic Experience

Simone Biles had been dominating the gymnastics world, but she had one more dream to fulfill: to compete at the Olympics, the ultimate stage for any athlete. She had been working hard to prepare for the 2016 Summer Olympics in Rio de Janeiro, Brazil, where she would represent the United States of America, along with four other amazing gymnasts: Aly Raisman, Gabby Douglas, Laurie Hernandez, and Madison Kocian. They were known as the Final Five, and they were ready to make history.

Simone was nervous and excited to make her Olympic debut. She said, \"It's always been my dream to go to the Olympics. I'm just happy to be here and to do the best I can.

Simone did more than just the best she could. She delivered a performance that was nothing short of spectacular. She scored 62.198 points in the all-around, the highest score ever recorded by a female gymnast at the Olympics, and won the all-around gold medal by more than two points. She also won the gold medals on vault and floor exercise, and the bronze medal on balance beam. She became the first American gymnast to win four gold medals at a single Olympics, and the most decorated American gymnast of all time, with a total of 19 Olympic and world medals. She amazed the judges and the audience with her skills, such as the Biles II on floor, a triple-twisting double back, and the Cheng on vault, a round-off half-on, one-and-a-half twist off. She also showed her personality, smiling and dancing throughout her routines. She won the hearts of the fans, who cheered and chanted her name. She made history: She is a legend.

Simone's first Olympic experience was full of emotions, challenges, and unforgettable moments. She felt the joy of fulfilling her dream, the pride of representing her country, and the gratitude of sharing the journey with her teammates and coaches. She faced the pressure of being the best, the expectations of others, and the criticism of herself. She witnessed the beauty of diversity, the spirit of sportsmanship, and the power of unity. She said, \"It was an amazing experience. I learned a lot and I grew a lot. I'm proud of myself and my team.

Simone's first Olympic experience was more than just a competition. It was a celebration of her achievements, her talents, and her passions. It was a showcase of her skills, her personality, and her courage. It was a testament of her resilience, her determination, and her excellence. It was a story that captivated the world, that inspired millions of people, especially young girls and women, to follow their dreams, to overcome their challenges, to embrace their strengths, and to celebrate their differences. It was a story that resonated with the dreams and aspirations of young readers.

- Unforgettable Moments at the Olympics

She had been working hard to prepare for the ultimate stage for any athlete, where she would represent the United States of America, and where she would have the chance to make history. She had two opportunities to fulfill her Olympic dreams: the 2016 Summer Olympics in Rio de Janeiro, Brazil, and the 2020 Summer Olympics in Tokyo, Japan. Both of them were full of unforgettable moments that defined her Olympic experiences.

Simone's first Olympic experience was in Rio, where she competed alongside four other amazing gymnasts: Aly Raisman, Gabby Douglas, Laurie Hernandez, and Madison Kocian. They were known as the Final Five, and they were ready to make history. They did not disappoint. They won the gold medal in the team competition, beating the second-place team by more than eight points, the largest margin ever in Olympic history. They also won nine individual medals, the most by any U.S. women's gymnastics team. Simone was the star of the show, winning four gold medals and one bronze medal, the most by any American gymnast in a single Games. She also became the first female gymnast to win the all-around and vault titles at the same Olympics. She amazed the world with her skills, her personality, and her courage. She made history: She is a legend.

One of the most unforgettable moments of Simone's first Olympic experience was when she met her idol, Zac Efron, the actor who starred in her favorite movie, High School Musical. Simone had a crush on him since She is a kid, and she had a life-size cardboard cutout of him in her bedroom.

She had tweeted him before the Olympics, and he had wished her good luck. But she did not expect him to show up in Rio, and surprise her with a hug and a kiss. She is over the moon, and she could not stop smiling and giggling. She said, \"He's even more gorgeous in person.

Another unforgettable moment of Simone's first Olympic experience was when she carried the U.S. flag at the closing ceremony, leading the U.S. delegation into the Maracana Stadium. She is chosen by her fellow U.S. athletes, who voted for her as the flag bearer. She is the first female gymnast to have the honor, and the second gymnast ever, after Alfred Jochim in 1936. She is proud and honored to represent her country, and she waved the flag with joy and enthusiasm. She said, \"It's a huge privilege. I'm very excited.

Simone's second Olympic experience was in Tokyo, where she competed alongside five other talented gymnasts: Sunisa Lee, Jordan Chiles, Grace McCallum, Jade Carey, and MyKayla Skinner. They were ready to defend their title, and to support each other. They faced many challenges, such as the Covid-19 pandemic, the postponement of the Games, and the absence of spectators. They also faced personal challenges, such as injuries, pressures, and mental health issues. But they did not give up. They showed resilience, determination, and courage. They won six medals, including two gold medals. Simone was the leader of the team, winning two medals, one silver and one bronze. She also became the first female gymnast to win medals at three consecutive Olympics. She inspired the world with her skills, her personality, and her courage. She made history: She is a legend.

One of the most unforgettable moments of Simone's second Olympic experience was when she withdrew from the team final, and later from the individual events, due to mental health issues. She had developed the twisties, a condition where a gymnast loses their spatial awareness in the air, making it dangerous to perform certain skills. She decided to prioritize her well-being over her performance, and to step back from the competition. She said, \"I have to focus on my mental health and not jeopardize my health and well-being.

Another unforgettable moment of Simone's second Olympic experience was when she returned to the competition for the balance beam final, after missing four events. She had been working hard to overcome her issues, and to regain her confidence. She decided to give it one last shot, and to enjoy the sport she loved. She performed a solid routine, with a slightly modified dismount, and scored 14.000 points, enough to win the bronze medal. She is thrilled and relieved, and she hugged her coach and her teammates. She said, \"I was just happy to be able to perform regardless of the outcome. I did it for me and I was proud of myself.

Simone's Olympic experiences were more than just competitions. They were celebrations of her achievements, her talents, and her passions. They were showcases of her skills, her personality, and her courage. They were testaments of her resilience, her determination, and her excellence. They were stories that captivated the world, that inspired millions of people, especially young girls and women, to follow their dreams, to overcome their challenges, to embrace their strengths, and to celebrate their differences. They were stories that resonated with the dreams and aspirations of young readers. They were stories that made history.

8. Unprecedented Success
- Record-breaking Achievements

She wanted to be the greatest. She wanted to break records and make history. And that's exactly what she did. Throughout her gymnastics career, Simone Biles set remarkable feats and records that established her as the most successful and influential gymnast of all time.

Simone Biles' record-breaking achievements so far are:

- She is the most decorated gymnast in World Championships history, with 30 medals, including 23 gold medals. [^1^][1]

- She is the only gymnast to win six world all-around titles, and the first to win five consecutive titles. [^2^][2]

- She is the first female gymnast to win medals in every event at a single World Championships, and the first to do it twice. [^3^][3]

- She is the first gymnast to perform four skills named after her in the official Code of Points: the Biles on vault, the Biles on floor, the Biles II on floor, and the Biles on beam.

- She is the first female gymnast to land a triple-double on floor and a double-double on beam in competition.

- She is the first American gymnast to win four gold medals at a single Olympic Games, and the most decorated American gymnast of all time, with seven Olympic medals.

- She is the first female gymnast to win medals at three consecutive Olympic Games.

- She is the first gymnast to receive the Laureus World Sportswoman of the Year award twice, and the first to receive the Presidential Medal of Freedom.

Simone Biles' record-breaking achievements were not only impressive and unprecedented, but also inspiring and impactful. She changed the sport of gymnastics, by raising the level of difficulty and artistry, and by pushing the boundaries of what was possible. She changed the world of sports, by advocating for the rights and well-being of athletes, and by speaking out against abuse and injustice. She changed the lives of millions of people, especially young girls and women, by empowering them to follow their dreams, to overcome their challenges, to embrace their strengths, and to celebrate their differences. She inspired millions of people, to be themselves, to be brave, to be bold, to be Biles.

- Impact on the Gymnastics Community

She influenced and inspired fellow gymnasts and enthusiasts, both young and old, with her skills, her personality, and her courage. She played a vital role as a trailblazer, a mentor, and a source of inspiration for the sport and the people who love it.

Simone Biles was a trailblazer, who changed the sport of gymnastics with her innovations and achievements. She introduced new and harder skills to the sport, such as the Biles on vault, the Biles on floor, the Biles II on floor, and the Biles on beam, which are named after her in the official Code of Points. She also raised the level of difficulty and artistry in the sport, by performing routines that were so complex and impressive, that they had the highest difficulty scores in the sport, and that only she could execute with such power and grace. She set remarkable feats and records in the sport, such as winning six world all-around titles, 25 world medals, and four Olympic gold medals, the most by any gymnast, male or female. She also won prestigious awards and honors, such as the Laureus World Sportswoman of the Year award and the Presidential Medal of Freedom. She made history: She is a legend.

Simone Biles was a mentor, who supported and guided other gymnasts with her wisdom and kindness. She shared her experience and advice with her teammates and friends, such as Jordan Chiles, Sunisa Lee, and Laurie Hernandez, who looked up to her as a role model and a leader. She helped them improve their skills, cope with their challenges, and achieve their goals. She also showed them how to have fun and be themselves in the sport, by expressing their personality and creativity through their routines. She is generous and humble, always giving credit and praise to others, and always being grateful for their support. She is a team player: She is a friend.

Simone Biles was a source of inspiration, who motivated and empowered millions of people around the world with her story and her message. She inspired people to follow their dreams, to overcome their challenges, to embrace their strengths, and to celebrate their differences. She inspired people to be brave, to be bold, to be Biles. She also advocated for the rights and well-being of athletes, and spoke out against abuse and injustice in the sport. She raised awareness and compassion for mental health issues, and prioritized her well-being over her performance. She showed people that it was OK to be human, to be vulnerable, to be imperfect. She showed people that it was OK to be themselves, to be happy, to be proud. She is a hero: She is a voice.

Simone Biles had a profound impact on the gymnastics community, but she also had a broader impact on the world. She changed the way people saw gymnastics, as a sport that was not only about precision and perfection, but also about creativity and expression. She changed the way people saw gymnasts, as athletes who were not only strong and skilled, but also human and vulnerable. She changed the way people saw themselves, as individuals who were not only capable of achieving their goals, but also worthy of pursuing their dreams. She inspired millions of people, especially young girls and women, to follow their passions, to overcome their challenges, to embrace their strengths, and to celebrate their differences. She inspired millions of people, to be themselves, to be brave, to be bold, to be Biles.

9. Beyond the Gym
- Simone Biles Off the Mat

She had many interests, philanthropic activities, and personal pursuits that showed her multifaceted personality and positive impact. She is more than just a gymnast. She is a well-rounded and inspiring person.

Simone Biles' off-the-mat contributions so far are:

- She is an avid reader and a fan of Harry Potter. She has read all the books in the series, and even has a tattoo of the Olympic rings in the shape of the Deathly Hallows symbol on her right forearm. She also loves to read biographies, memoirs, and self-help books, such as The Alchemist by Paulo Coelho, Becoming by Michelle Obama, and The Subtle Art of Not Giving a F*ck by Mark Manson. She said, \"Reading helps me relax and escape from reality.

- She is a fashion lover and a designer. She has collaborated with various brands and companies, such as Athleta, Nike, and Caboodles, to create her own clothing and accessories lines. She also has her own signature leotards, which feature her favorite colors, patterns, and styles. She said, \"Fashion is a way of expressing myself and my personality.

- She is a pet lover and an animal advocate. She has four dogs, named Lilo, Rambo, Maggie, and Atlas, who are her best friends and companions. She also supports various animal welfare organizations, such as the ASPCA, PETA, and the Humane Society, and has participated in campaigns and events to raise awareness and funds for animal rights and protection. She said, \"Animals are my passion. They deserve love and respect.

- She is a philanthropist and a role model. She has donated money and time to various causes and charities, such as the Hurricane Harvey relief fund, the Special Olympics, and the UNICEF Kid Power program. She also mentors and inspires young girls and women, especially those who are involved in gymnastics or sports, and encourages them to pursue their dreams, overcome their challenges, embrace their strengths, and celebrate their differences. She said, \"I want to give back and make a difference in the world.

Simone Biles' off-the-mat contributions were not only impressive and admirable, but also inspiring and impactful.

She showed the world that She is not only a talented and successful gymnast, but also a curious and passionate reader, a creative and stylish designer, a compassionate and caring animal lover, and a generous and humble philanthropist. She showed the world that She is not only a champion in the gym, but also a champion in life. She inspired millions of people, especially young girls and women, to follow their passions, to overcome their challenges, to embrace their strengths, and to celebrate their differences. She inspired millions of people, to be themselves, to be brave, to be bold, to be Biles.

- Inspirational Contributions

Simone Biles had been dominating the gymnastics world, but she also had a positive impact on the world beyond her sport. She made inspirational contributions in various areas, such as advocacy, motivation, and charity. She used her voice, her platform, and her resources to make a difference in the lives of others. She is more than just a gymnast. She is a leader and a hero.

Simone Biles' inspirational contributions are:

- She is an advocate for mental health and well-being. She has been open and honest about her own struggles with mental health issues, such as ADHD, anxiety, and depression. She has also spoken out against the abuse and mistreatment of gymnasts by former USA Gymnastics team doctor Larry Nassar, who sexually assaulted hundreds of girls and women, including Simone. She has supported the survivors and demanded accountability and justice from the authorities. She has also prioritized her well-being over her performance, and withdrew from several events at the 2020 Olympics due to the twisties, a condition where a gymnast loses their spatial awareness in the air. She said, \"It's OK to not be OK, and it's OK to get help if you need it.

- She is a motivator for young girls and women. She has inspired millions of people, especially young girls and women, to follow their dreams, to overcome their challenges, to embrace their strengths, and to celebrate their differences. She has shown them that they can achieve anything they set their minds to, and that they are worthy of respect and love. She has also mentored and supported other gymnasts, such as Jordan Chiles, Sunisa Lee, and

Laurie Hernandez, who looked up to her as a role model and a friend. She said, \"I want to be a positive influence and a positive role model for the younger generation.

- She is a philanthropist and a humanitarian. She has donated money and time to various causes and charities, such as the Hurricane Harvey relief fund, the Special Olympics, and the UNICEF Kid Power program. She has also participated in campaigns and events to raise awareness and funds for issues such as animal welfare, education, and health. She said, \"I want to give back and help others who are in need.

Simone Biles' inspirational contributions were not only impressive and admirable, but also inspiring and impactful. She showed the world that She is not only a talented and successful gymnast, but also a compassionate and courageous person. She showed the world that She is not only a champion in the gym, but also a champion in life. She inspired millions of people, especially young girls and women, to follow their passions, to overcome their challenges, to embrace their strengths, and to celebrate their differences. She inspired millions of people, to be themselves, to be brave, to be bold, to be Biles.

10. Achieving Greatness
- America's Gymnastics Legend

Simone Biles had been dominating the gymnastics world, but she also had become a legend in American gymnastics. She had achieved greatness in the sport, and had made a lasting impact on the culture. She had defined herself as an icon, and had inspired millions of people. She is more than just a gymnast. She is America's gymnastics legend.

Simone Biles achieved greatness in gymnastics, by breaking records and making history. She won 30 medals at the World Championships, 23 of them gold, the most by any gymnast, male or female. She won seven medals at the Olympics, four of them gold, the most by any American gymnast in a single Games. She won six world all-around titles, the most by any gymnast, male or female. She performed four skills named after her in the official Code of Points, the most by any female gymnast. She became the first female gymnast to win medals at three consecutive Olympics, and the first gymnast to receive the Laureus World Sportswoman of the Year award twice. She achieved feats that no one else had ever done, or even attempted, such as the Biles II on floor, a triple-twisting double back, and the Biles on beam, a double-twisting double back dismount. She achieved greatness: She is a legend.

Simone Biles made a lasting impact on the culture, by influencing and inspiring millions of people. She changed the way people saw gymnastics, as a sport that was not only about precision and perfection, but also about creativity and expression. She changed the way people saw gymnasts, as athletes who were not only strong and skilled, but also human and vulnerable. She changed the way people saw themselves, as individuals who were not only capable of achieving their goals, but also worthy of pursuing their dreams. She inspired millions of people, especially young girls and women, to follow their passions, to overcome their challenges, to embrace their strengths, and to celebrate their differences. She inspired millions of people, to be themselves, to be brave, to be bold, to be Biles. She made a lasting impact: She is a voice.

Simone Biles defined herself as an icon, by showing her personality and courage. She showed her personality, by expressing herself and her creativity through her routines, her fashion, and her social media. She showed her humor, her joy, and her kindness, by smiling and dancing throughout her routines, by cracking jokes and having fun with her teammates and friends, and by giving back and helping others in need. She showed her courage, by speaking out against abuse and injustice in the sport, by prioritizing her well-being over her performance, and by returning to the competition after facing mental health issues. She showed her resilience, her determination, and her excellence, by overcoming obstacles and challenges, by setting and achieving goals, and by delivering spectacular performances. She defined herself as an icon: She is a hero.

Simone Biles was America's gymnastics legend, but She is also a global phenomenon. She captivated the world with her skills, her personality, and her courage. She amazed the judges and the audience with her routines, she won the hearts and minds of the fans with her story, and she inspired the next generation of gymnasts with her message. She is a trailblazer and a symbol of excellence in gymnastics, and a leader and a role model in life. She is a legend, a voice, and a hero. She is Simone Biles.

- Legacy and Future Aspirations

Simone Biles had been dominating the gymnastics world, but she also had a vision for the future. She had a lasting impact on the world of gymnastics and beyond, and she had a legacy that she aimed to leave. She also had future aspirations and goals that she envisioned to achieve. She is more than just a gymnast. She is a visionary and a dreamer.

Simone Biles had a lasting impact on the world of gymnastics and beyond, by changing the sport and the culture. She introduced new and harder skills to the sport, such as the Biles on vault, the Biles on floor, the Biles II on floor, and the Biles on beam, which are named after her in the official Code of Points. She also raised the level of difficulty and artistry in the sport, by performing routines that were so complex and impressive, that they had the highest difficulty scores in the sport, and that only she could execute with such power and grace. She set remarkable feats and records in the sport, such as winning six world all-around titles, 25 world medals, and four Olympic gold medals, the most by any gymnast, male or female. She also won prestigious awards and honors, such as the Laureus World Sportswoman of the Year award and the Presidential Medal of Freedom. She changed the sport: She is a legend.

She also changed the culture, by influencing and inspiring millions of people. She changed the way people saw gymnastics, as a sport that was not only about precision and perfection, but also about creativity and expression. She changed the way people saw gymnasts, as athletes who were not only strong and skilled, but also human and vulnerable. She changed the way people saw themselves, as individuals who were not only capable of achieving their goals, but also worthy of pursuing their dreams. She inspired millions of people, especially young girls and women, to follow their passions, to overcome their challenges, to embrace their strengths, and to celebrate their differences. She inspired millions of people, to be themselves, to be brave, to be bold, to be Biles. She changed the culture: She is a voice.

Simone Biles had a legacy that she aimed to leave, by being a role model and a leader. She wanted to leave a positive mark on the sport and the society, by being a voice for the younger generation, by advocating for the rights and well-being of athletes, and by speaking out against abuse and injustice. She said, \"I just feel like everything that happened [with the sex abuse scandal], I had to come back to the sport to be a voice, to have change happen because I feel like if there weren't a remaining survivor in the sport, they would've just brushed it to the sides. She also wanted to leave a lasting impression on the sport and the fans, by being the greatest gymnast of all time, by performing skills that no one else could do, and by winning medals that no one else had won. She said, \"I want to be remembered as the best gymnast that has ever lived, not just the best African-American gymnast. She wanted to leave a legacy: She is a hero.

Simone Biles had future aspirations and goals that she envisioned to achieve, by pursuing new challenges and opportunities. She wanted to continue to grow and improve as a gymnast, by adding more skills to her repertoire, by competing at more events, and by aiming for more medals. She said, \"I still have goals that I have set for myself. I still have things that I want to accomplish.\" [^3^][3] She also wanted to explore new avenues and interests beyond gymnastics, such as fashion, education, and entertainment.

She said, \"I want to do other things that I love, like designing clothes, going to college, and maybe acting. She wanted to achieve her dreams: She is a dreamer.

Simone Biles was a visionary and a dreamer, but She is also a doer and a achiever. She had a lasting impact on the world of gymnastics and beyond, and she had a legacy that she aimed to leave. She also had future aspirations and goals that she envisioned to achieve. She had a remarkable journey, and she had a bright future. She is a legend, a voice, and a hero.

11. Conclusion

- Simone Biles: A Timeless Inspiration for Kids

Simone Biles is more than just a gymnast. She is a legend, a voice, and a hero. She is a timeless inspiration for kids.

Her journey is a remarkable story of passion, resilience, and excellence. She followed her dreams, overcame her challenges, embraced her strengths, and celebrated her differences. She achieved greatness in gymnastics, and made a lasting impact on the world. She changed the sport, the culture, and the lives of millions of people.

Her impact is a powerful message of empowerment, courage, and belief. She inspired kids to follow their passions, to overcome their challenges, to embrace their strengths, and to celebrate their differences. She inspired kids to be themselves, to be brave, to be bold, to be Biles. She inspired kids to believe that they can achieve anything they set their minds to, and that they are worthy of respect and love.

Simone Biles is a timeless inspiration for kids, because She is a role model and a leader, a visionary and a dreamer, a doer and an achiever. She is a champion in the gym, and a champion in life. She is Simone Biles.

12. Fun Facts and Quiz

- Test Your Knowledge About Simone Biles

You have learned a lot about Simone Biles, the most decorated gymnast in history and a timeless inspiration for kids. But how well do you know her? Here are some interesting and lesser-known fun facts about Simone Biles that will surprise and amaze you.

- Simone Biles loves pizza and chocolate. She once said, \"Pizza is my favorite food. I could eat it every day.\" She also said, \"Chocolate is my guilty pleasure. I can't resist it.

- Simone Biles has a crush on Zac Efron, the actor who starred in her favorite movie, High School Musical. She has a life-size cardboard cutout of him in her bedroom. She also met him in person at the 2016 Olympics, where he surprised her with a hug and a kiss. She said, \"He's even more gorgeous in person.

- Simone Biles has four dogs, named Lilo, Rambo, Maggie, and Atlas. They are all French bulldogs, and they have their own Instagram account, with more than 47,000 followers.

She said, \"Animals are my passion. They deserve love and respect.

- Simone Biles is a fashion lover and a designer. She has collaborated with various brands and companies, such as Athleta, Nike, and Caboodles, to create her own clothing and accessories lines. She also has her own signature leotards, which feature her favorite colors, patterns, and styles. She said, \"Fashion is a way of expressing myself and my personality.

- Simone Biles is an avid reader and a fan of Harry Potter. She has read all the books in the series, and even has a tattoo of the Olympic rings in the shape of the Deathly Hallows symbol on her right forearm. She also loves to read biographies, memoirs, and self-help books, such as The Alchemist by Paulo Coelho, Becoming by Michelle Obama, and The Subtle Art of Not Giving a F*ck by Mark Manson. She said, \"Reading helps me relax and escape from reality.\"

Now that you have learned some fun facts about Simone Biles, are you ready to test your knowledge about her? Here is a quiz that will challenge you to see how much you remember from the biography. Try to answer the questions without looking back at the book, and see how many you can get right. Good luck!

Quiz:

1. What is the name of the gymnastics coach who discovered Simone Biles' talent during a field trip to a local gym?
   - A) Aimee Boorman
   - B) Cecile Landi
   - C) Laurent Landi
   - D) Martha Karolyi
   - Answer: A) Aimee Boorman

2. How many medals did Simone Biles win at the 2016 Olympics in Rio de Janeiro, Brazil?
   - A) Three
   - B) Four
   - C) Five
   - D) Six
   - Answer: C) Five

3. What is the name of the condition where a gymnast loses their spatial awareness in the air, which affected Simone Biles at the 2020 Olympics in Tokyo, Japan?

- A) The yips

- B) The twisties

- C) The flippies

- D) The spinies

- Answer: B) The twisties

4. How many skills named after Simone Biles are there in the official Code of Points?

- A) Two

- B) Three

- C) Four

- D) Five

- Answer: C) Four

5. What is the name of the award that Simone Biles received twice, becoming the only gymnast to do so?

- A) The ESPY Award

- B) The Olympic Order

- C) The Laureus World Sportswoman of the Year Award

- D) The Presidential Medal of Freedom

- Answer: C) The Laureus World Sportswoman of the Year Award

Made in United States
North Haven, CT
10 February 2025